Book of Poems and Prayer for All Seasons

James Al Reas

WORKBOOK PRESS LLC
187 E Warm Springs Rd,
Suite B285 Las Vegas NV 89119 USA

Website: https://workbookpress.com/
Hotline: 1-888-818-4856
Email: admin@workbookpress.com

Ordering Information:

Quantity sales. Special discounts are available on quantity purchases by corporations, associations, and others. For details, contact the publisher at the address above.

Library of Congress Control Number:

ISBN-13:   978-1-961845-43-5   Paperback Version
               978-1-961845-52-7   Digital Version

REV. DATE: 07/12/2024

BOOK of POEMS
and PRAYER for
ALL SEASONS

James Al Reas

Table Of Contents

Father Ives Place

by James Al Reas©

There is a place where one can live,
With homely joy, no one can give. . .
It is a place in San Jose,
On a quiet street called Sage Wood Lane.

Many a party had been made,
The weekends lively with food and drinks . . .
A fountain flows a bird would feed,
Even on winter's coldest eve.

The lawns are green, the flowers fresh.
Despite a scorching summer heat
It soothes the pain and quench the spirit,
Through life's long journey to the end.

I love to live in San Jose,
As long as heavens wants me to be . . .
But time must change as mortals fade
Into its unknown destiny.

I love to stay in San Jose,
A shepherd's house for you and me . . .
No one can break its mystery,
A silent whisper might one day.

I shall now end this simple piece,
Like summer wind a gentle breeze . . .
There is no house you will ever live, Father Ives place
Where life whirls in its sweetness and in pain.

The Golden Year

by James Al Reas©

Fifty long years of marriage, the Golden Year a turning point.
Hard to reach almost impossible to achieve,
Few would sometimes ever believe.

We thank the Lord for his kindness, the wonderful blessings,
Our children and grandchildren...
The chance to live, enjoy marriage life to the fullest.

Many a marriage didn't last, they were broken they were split...
After so many years at times, even less than a year.
Lucky are those who would survive; "The Greatest test of all time."

Marriage is a vow a covenant a life, long adventure.
To have and to hold, for better for worse, for richer for poorer...
In sickness and in health, to love and to cherish till death.

Such, is the binding ancient sacred oath,
the very basic foundation of matrimony.
It is further written; "What God has joined together,
let no man put asunder."
Ignore the law and life, will never be the same again.

We are now in the autumn of this borrowed life.
A few more years or maybe tomorrow, a marker,
An inscription in a desolate lonely place would sadly read,
"In Loving Memory."
A faint reminder of someone's previous mortal existence.

In our lifetime, we may not be the best of parents...
But somehow, we tried, lived, and walked closer to it.
What act of love, compassion, and generosity...
Can one further bestow.

When the journey is over, and the trumpets of victory are played...
We will be happy to look back, revisit,
The many trying and exciting years we hurdled together.
Remarkably, this Golden Year is the Best Year of Our Life.

To our family, relatives and friends.
We deeply treasure those golden moments and happy days,
once shared together.
Wish it would never end. May the gift of Love, Peace and Harmony,
Dwell and settle down in the deepest chambers of your hearts forever.

The Power of Love

by James Al Reas©

The power of love is like the sun that shines forever.
You ask me when it will end…I'll tell you never.

You need me as I need you, as roses need the rain.
I love you as you love me, from this day until eternity.

As the years goes by, let our love grow and flourish…
Every second, every minute, every hour, day by day.

Promise me, you will never change.
In good or bad times, in victory or defeat, in sickness and in health

Know that this world…is full of treachery, lies, betrayals and deceit.
The greatest thing we will ever learn is just to
love and be loved in return.
"To quote a line from a favorite song by: Natalie Cole"

Life And Death Its Beauty And Dignity

by James Al Reas©

It is written..." Come to me all ye that labor and are heavily
burdened and I will give you rest."

Here lies a man, who once walked, lived, and worked with us.

An honorable being who just passed on to the other world,
a world unknown, mysterious, intriguing.

The shadow of his life, the imprint of his footprints....

The fond memories of his warmth company will forever
linger deep down in the bottom of our hearts.

Death is like a thief in the night. It strikes the rich,
the famous and the royalties.

It demolishes and annihilates the good, the bad and the ugly.

Death has no tolerance or distinction...for the young and the old,

Man or woman, race, and color...even ethnic origin.

Everything in this world has its own beginning;
it also has its tragic end at times.

Atlantis the lost continent, the Mayan Civilization...
the Pharaohs of Egypt, the Roman Empire, to name a few.

In their own time they were legends, walked through this world
with all glory, riches, grandeur, and splendor.

When their time came, they just vanished and disappear...
like a song that has lost its meaning, appeal, and popularity.

If there is such a thing as beauty in living...
there is also that honor and dignity in dying.

Man should therefore overcome and face tomorrow,
never ever afraid of the reality of death.

TO THE WOMAN I LOVE

by James Al Reas©

To the woman I love Celestina.
I promised myself never to love again,
Until the day you came along.
I see your face in every woman I met . . .
I see your smile in every flower that blossoms,
I hear your voice in the stillness of the night . . .
Deep in my heart I must confess,
I am deeply in love with you.

We live in two different worlds,
So diverse so far apart . . .
More than we could ever imagine.
You had your share of troubles and trials . . .
As much as I had mine.
I carried scars of great anguish,
From a distant past lived with the pain . . .
Never really learned to live alone.

I crave for a warmth company.
I thirst for a loving care,
I need your soft caress . . .
And longed for your embrace.
I was blind to have adored you,
Enchanted by your irresistible charm . . .
Just human enough to be a slave,
Too weak and helpless to resist.

I want to walk with you,
On a sudden summer rain.
Hug you on the first day of spring . . .
Be with you on a cold winter night,

Dance with you . . .
One enchanted evening,
To the sweet melody of the song . . .
"Somewhere Over the Rainbow."

To the woman I love Celestina.
How I wish you were just a dream,
That my thoughts will be free again . . .
At the early break of dawn.
I was a fool to think I could fall in love,
And my heart would never ever cry again.
Please, let me live in this world, and die with dignity,
In pursuit of an honorable and undying love for you.

FOREVER YOUNG

by James AL Reas©

Forever young, forever young, forever young.
It could be a wildest dream, a wishful thinking . . .
An escape from harsh reality, an illusion of living far beyond . . .
The essence of human mortality.

As you reach eighteen, it's that turning point of your life . . .
When you reach adolescence, the period when
everything in this world . . .
Will suddenly and finally change.

The way you look, the way you feel . . . the way you act.
The way you look at your friends,
The way you look at life.

Henceforth, you begin to appreciate,
the real meaning and beauty of nature . . .
The wonderful sight of every flower that blossoms,
the chirping of birds at the early break of dawn . . .
The rainbow in the sky, after a sudden summer rain.

As you embark on your long journey in life,
be strong, brave and courageous.
Follow your dreams, reach for your goals,
no matter how far, no matter how hard . . .
No matter how hopeless, to quote a line from a famous song.

Preach only love, when you preach love,
you will never think of deception . . .
You will never think of destruction. When you preach love,
You fill people's hearts with joy, God will bless you, for God is Love.

In revisiting the happy childhood of yesteryears, reach out to the most
powerful God, of all creations,
Ask Him to preserve your youthful looks and beauty . . .
Make your life and all those who turned eighteen today,
Forever young, forever young, forever young,

Yesterday

by James Al Reas©

Yesterday has gone away,
Never to return in anyway.
Yesterday has gone away,
Sweet and bitter memories remain in me.

Yesterday has gone away,
A moment past a lifelong journey,
A song that reached the height of day...
Slowly fades and dies away.

Yesterday has gone away,
Strange reflection of destiny.
A flower bloomed but never blossomed,
Dreams that never saw the light of day.

Yesterday has gone away,
When we can give something to the needy...
When we can share a little of our blessings,
When we can manage a smile,
Although our hearts are on fire.

Yesterday has gone away,
If we can appreciate the beauty of today.
Live in love, peace, and harmony,
For today is tomorrow...
After tomorrow,
Only yesterday.

Friendly Persuasion

by James Al Reas©

Deep in our hearts,
We had known the word love
Quite a very long while,
For a very intricate reason . . .
We called it friendship.

We ignored and camouflaged,
The delicate feeling of love.
With subtle ways of pretense,
False appearance and secrecy . . .
We tried to break destroy and bury.

As the years go by,
Behind that friendship . . .
Is a love that bloomed
but never blossomed like a dream . . .
That never saw the light of day.

No matter how we tried,
Love refused to die . . .
Like a grain of plant seed
That grows and germinates in an open field . . .
Nourished by the watering rain . . .
Caressed by the warm touch of the sun.

Tears of Goodbye

by James Al Reas©

Into each life a tear must fall.
Tears of Love and Hatred,
Tears of Joy and Sorrow . . .
Tears of Victory or Defeat.
Tears of Pain and Suffering.
In my long life's journey,
I have seen them all.

Nothing comes close however,
To that tragic moment when I saw those teardrops . . .
Rolling slowly down her eyes.
Oozing gently on her lovely countenance.
Her last tears of sad goodbye.

Not the very tears we have in common,
Something more real, more touching.
More moving, more heartbreaking.
It transcends to the very essence of human existence,
It's indelible mark of mortality.

Those were the tears of death,
The last teardrops coming out . . .
From someone's physical being.
As we pass on to the other world,
A world unknown, a world of no return.

Body still, cold, immobile, almost lifeless,
Strange mysterious feeling . . .
Shook the very core of my whole being.
Something different, something unusual.
Something unreal.

Deep in my heart I knew,
Those were the very teardrops.
Most precious tears unfolding . . .
Last tears of the final moments,
Of her last breath on earth.
Her last tears of goodbye.

Into Each Life Some Rain Must Fall

by James Al Reas©

Into each life some rain must fall,
Into each plant a leaf or a flower.

Into each birth a mother and a father . . .
Humans, Animals, Reptiles, Birds, and Insects.
Useless each without the other . . .
All are God's creation.

We are in a journey of life, which could be long or short . . .
Rough or easy, human endurance will be at play.

We undergo pleasures and pain,
There will be sunshine and rain.
Whatever happens . . .
Man should learn to stand once again.

If we survived all the tests,
The stumbling blocks . . .
And finally succeeded,
There's still that element of human mortality.
We had to deal with.

You can rebuke and say . . .
For you, dreadful death,
Die in the flower of youth . . .
And visit us no more.

We can only dream, for a long and happy life . . .
But only God can make it happen.

Prayer for All Seasons

by James Al Reas©

Dear Lord, I come to you today with great faith, enthusiasm, humbleness and humility. I ask forgiveness for my human shortcomings and my inequities. Let me walk with confidence and peace of mind in your ways and in the shadow and grace of your divine love and mercy.

Please give me the strength and courage to carry on my unwavering trust and belief in you. Let me not falter even in times of trials, tribulations and distress. As we persevere and pursue our dreams in this lifelong journey in search for greener pastures, please secure our safety and protect our families from harm.

Always remind us to look back from where we came from and extend our helping hand to the less fortunate. Bless the sick and the suffering, heal their bodies and make them whole again. Life is too short for them to be denied of the pleasures, enjoyments and opportunities.

For our departed loved ones, let them rest in peace knowing that they will never be forgotten forever deep within our hearts. Dear Lord, I know you can do anything in your power even the most hopeless and impossible, please bring that heavenly gift of providence and miracle into my life.

Thank you so much for being my God, who sees my every need. Thank you so much for being there for me in good or bad times when I needed you most. May the gift of LOVE, PEACE and HARMONY, forever dwell and settle down in the deepest chambers our hearts for the rest of our lives.

Dear Lord, please make this world a better place to live in for us and for all humanity. In Jesus' name I pray, amen.

12/09/17